Table of Contents

Introduction

Life is pleasant. Death is peaceful. It's the transition that's troublesome.
–Issac Asimov, author

The interval between the decay of the old and the formation and establishment of the new constitutes a period of transition which must always necessarily be one of uncertainty, confusion, error, and wild and fierce fanaticism.
-John C. Calhoun, "A Disquisition on Government," 1851

The United States has been in a perpetual state of conflict since 11 September 2001 with Operations Enduring Freedom and New Dawn.[1] As Operation Enduring Freedom continues, the United States is entering its twelfth year of conflict—the longest in the country's history—with al-Qa'ida and its affiliates, and recently concluded Operation New Dawn on 14 December 2011 after eight years of conflict in Iraq.[2] The national leadership identified specific end states and objectives at the conclusion of each campaign. For Iraq, the strategy focused on "an Iraq that is sovereign, stable, and self-reliant."[3] Similarly, the strategy in Afghanistan relies on developing "self-reliant Afghan security forces" and an effective Afghan government.[4] Through these similar ends, the United States desires a strategic partnership with both the Iraqi and Afghan governments to strengthen U.S. national security further. Both approaches require the cessation of military-led operations and a transition to civilian-led diplomatic relationships. As the U.S.

---

[1] Preceded by Operation Iraqi Freedom, Operation New Dawn started on 1 September 2010 and marked the end of U.S. military combat operations in Iraq on 31 August 2010. Operation Iraqi Freedom covered 19 March 2003–31 August 2010.

[2] Barack Obama, Remarks by the President and First Lady on the End of the War in Iraq, (Fort Bragg, North Carolina. 14 December 2011). http://www.whitehouse.gov/the-press-office/2011/12/14/remarks-president-and-first-lady-end-war-iraq (14 January 2012).

[3] Barack Obama, "Responsibly Ending the War in Iraq," in *Remarks of President Barack Obama* (Camp Lejeune, North Carolina: 27 February 2009).

[4] United States Government, "White Paper of the Interagency Policy Group's Report on U.S. Policy toward Afghanistan and Pakistan." http://www.whitehouse.gov/assets/documents/afghanistan _pakistan_white_paper_final.pdf (5 November 2011).

approaches the conclusion of Operation Enduring Freedom, it is important to remember this is not the first time the United States encountered this problem of transition from military-led operations to civilian-led diplomatic relationships. The United States' history of conflicts and transitions is important today as it approaches the closure of Operation Enduring Freedom. Although thoughts about why war starts and how they are conducted change over time, the use of military means to achieve political ends has always been a constant. Many military theorists from Sun Tzu to Machiavelli to Clausewitz have identified this immutable principle of war, so understanding how to link them is of importance to military planners.

The transition is one of the most important parts of any campaign linking military means to achieve political ends, but it is also one of the most overlooked elements. Much of the intellectual discussion focuses on actions that occur either before or after a transition. Military discussions revolve around reforming doctrine to conduct offensive, defensive, or stability operations effectively while civilian discourse looks at new government structures or expanding civilian authorities. The civil-military realm focuses on interagency processes or whole-of-government approaches to improve functionality to the government's approach to conflict. However, most of the discussion avoids the mechanism to link all these different elements, leading to the question: How does the United States military set conditions to successfully transition responsibility from military-led operations to civilian-led relationships?

This monograph argues early planning, interactive and iterative discourse between military planners and civilian officials, and continuous refinements establish the conditions to successfully transition military-led operations to a civilian-led diplomatic relationship. It provides a historical context for post-conflict planning considerations and successful transitions. Case studies and the process tracing methodology form the core of the monograph and should reveal three primary characteristics: level of post-conflict planning prior to the conclusion of military operations, the importance of dialogue between military and civilian leadership, and transition criteria. First, the level of post-conflict planning is the extent of planning conducted prior to conflict termination and the timeframe involved. Interagency dialogue identifies the level of civilian considerations in post-conflict planning to include direct coordination and cooperation between military and civilian leadership. Finally, transition criteria will compare and contrast the necessary conditions identified by planners to evolve from military-led to civilian-led operations successfully. The cause and effect link in the evidence should reveal that early planning facilitates an open and iterative dialogue between military planners and civilian officials. This discourse then reveals the necessary requirements and end state conditions to transition operations from the military to civilian agencies. As conditions and requirements change, planners are able to make refinements to the plan, thus allowing for a successful transition later. The efficacy of this methodology is it uses historical examples to identify situations that are analogous to today's planning dilemmas for post-conflict operations.

Four main sections partition the following analysis. The first section is a literature review identifying the different approaches military, civilian, and civil-military relations communities propose as possible solutions. This section will identify their utility and limitations as well as defining transitions. After the literature review, the analysis examines key historical case studies. World War II (Operation Eclipse) and the Vietnam War (Vietnamization and CORDS) are the two primary examples, but the analysis uses an additional case study—Operations Just Cause and Promote Liberty—to emphasize key points. [5] The third section expands upon the principles of successful transitions identified in the previous section. Finally, the analysis will then allow recommendations for improving efforts in future conflict to ensure planners incorporate transitions into the campaign design effectively.

---

[5] CORDS stands for the Civil Operations and Revolutionary Development Support Program.

Enabling a Successful Transition

Concepts such as whole of government approaches, interagency cooperation, and independent, military-led government institutions enter the discussion as ways to facilitate effective transitions. Although these ideas contribute to successful civilian-led diplomatic relationships in a post-conflict environment, the majority of the discourse neglects how to integrate and implement these concepts effectively, if at all, in the absence of new or revised structures. In other words, the many theories address either the lack of capacity (e.g., military personnel trained in economic theory) or the lack of capability (e.g., the need for an interagency command and control structure), but do not address the mechanism to translate new or existing capacities and capabilities into success.

To appreciate the debate fully, the definition of *transition* underpins any discussion of potential opportunities, recommendations, and conclusions. According to Joint Publication 5-0, transitions are distinct shifts in focus by the joint force, often accompanied by changes in command or support relationships.[6] Since the analysis concentrates on the change from military-led operations to civilian-led diplomatic relationships, one must realize it is more than just a shift in focus; it is also a distinct shift in effort. This combination between *focus* and *effort* is important because the shift is more than just a matter of a concentration of ideas, but exertion of energies and resources. Therefore, for the purposes of this analysis, the definition of a transition is as a point in time in which a distinct shift in focus and effort is required to achieve strategic ends. The conceptual debate that frames a transition focuses on the synergistic effect between military and civilian agencies.

---

[6] Joint Publication 5-0 (JP 5-0), III-40.

4

Interagency cooperation is not a new concept, but a resurgent focus on interagency processes resurfaced because of the emphasis on counterinsurgency and stability operations in recent years. Bob Ulin, CEO of the CGSC Foundation, Inc., describes that the "lack [of a system] to ensure effective interagency coordination poses a challenge."[7] Ulin also goes on to state that "there is little incentive to cooperate" between different governmental agencies because of "the difficulty, if not the inability, to delegate authority below the Presidential level across department and agency borders."[8] This lack of incentive and systems incites the discourse on how to increase the effectiveness of interagency cooperation. Among the different ideas on how to increase this efficiency, the more prevalent ones revolve around changing the physical structure of interagency or expanding its authority to produce unity of effort.

Changing the interagency structure takes on many forms, but the central idea is to introduce a new structure, such as command and control structure or a subordinate organization, or a new policy or regulation that increases the efficiency of the interagency system. An example of a new structure is a Joint Interagency Coordination Group (JIACG). They originated out of the need to support Department of Defense counterterrorism missions as directed by the President of the United States after the 11 September attack "to plan and execute counterterrorist activities jointly and fully share information and intelligence."[9] Joint Interagency Coordination Groups are subordinate organizations within geographic combatant commands, and according to Jan Schwarzenberg, two of the more important elements to ensure their success were the "status and

---

[7] Bob Ulin, "About Interagency Cooperation," *Interagency Essay*, no. 10-01 (September 2010). http://thesimonscenter.org/wp-content/uploads/2010/09/IAE-10-01.pdf (accessed August 4, 2011), 2.

[8] Ibid.

[9]Jan Schwarzenberg, "Where are the JIACGs Today?," *Interagency Journal* 2, no. 2 (Summer 2011), 24.

rank of the JIACG leaders, and secondly, to whom the JIACG reported."[10] These groups eventually led the way to similar structures such as the Commander's Interagency Engagement Group and the Joint Interagency Task Force at Umm Qasr, Iraq, as examples.

Administrative proposals such as legislation or expanding the authority of current leadership positions are much more theoretical at this point. For example, Congressman Randy Forbes introduced legislation titled, "The Interagency Cooperation Commission Act" on 30 April 2009 and the purpose was "to examine the long-term global challenges facing the United States and develop legislative and administrative proposals to improve interagency cooperation."[11] However, the furthest this legislation went was a referral on 29 June 2009 to the House Subcommittee on Government Management, Organization, and Procurement.[12] Others such as Christopher Lamb and Edward Marks "argue that the interagency integration problem can be rectified by expanding the President's power to delegate a modified 'chief of mission' authority similar to that granted ambassadors to oversee and direct the activities of employees from diverse government organizations."[13] President Eisenhower initiated the first attempts to empower and codify chief of mission authority in 1951 when he established the original predecessor to modern day country teams in which Eisenhower tasked the chiefs of mission "to exercise full responsibility for the direction, coordination, and supervision of all executive branch U.S. offices

---

[10] Ibid., 25.

[11] Ulin, "About Interagency Cooperation," 4. The number of the act is H.R. 2207, 111th Congress.

[12] http://thomas.loc.gov/cgi-bin/bdquery/z?d111:HR02207:@@@L&summ2=m& (accessed 11 November 2011).

[13] Christopher Lamb and Edward Marks, "Expanding Chief of Mission Authority to Produce Unity of Effort," *Interagency Essay*, no. 11-02 (May 2011). http://thesimonscenter.org/wp-content/uploads/2011/05/IAE-11-02-MAY2011.pdf (accessed August 4, 2011), 2.

and personnel."[14] Although both suggestions (changing the physical structure and expanding authorities) achieved limited successes independently in the past, the two are interdependent and the problems to change each independently are twofold.

First, a structure change to the interagency process alone does not bring about a desire to cooperate because a sense of community does not equate to an increase in cooperation.[15] The design of interagency structures, whether ad hoc like the interagency task force for Umm Qasr or established like combatant command JIACGs, are to create a sense of community by bringing together people of different backgrounds and specialties under an auspice of a common goal. These different agencies organized under a shared command and control structure develop trust between the different agencies so that one agency does not feel overshadowed or bullied by another. However, this is not the case because William Davis states, "There is a minimal correlation between a psychological [sense of community] and the importance of the joint, own service, or interagency communities."[16] He goes on to say the "effectiveness of ad hoc operations…that require various agencies to work together on a moment's notice does not rely on members of those agencies having developed a rich sense of community."[17] These statements indicate that the most important aspect to create unity of effort physical structure is not how the interagency structure is organized.

---

[14] Ibid., 5.

[15] William J Davis, "Is a Sense of Community Vital to Interagency Coordination?," *Interagency Paper*, no. 3 (January 2011): 2-3. Davis cites Sense of Community Theory as the theory to which practitioners, educators, and trainers should look for guidance in order to ensure that a "whole of government" approach to solving complex contingencies is optimized. Sense of Community Theory is comprised of four components: spirit, trust, trade, and art. Davis assumes that an application of the Sense of Community Theory to the task of improving interagency cooperation and coordination could be useful, if not critical.

[16] Ibid., 9.

[17] Ibid.

Second, an expansion of authorities requires legislative and administrative changes that do not clarify ambiguous interpretation of those policies. Lamb and Marks state that from 1951 "there has been some ambiguity over the interpretation of the extent of the executive authority being delegated."[18] They go on to explain that "other departments and agencies … have questioned … the practical application of chief of mission authority" and this is "especially true with those departments who also conduct extensive foreign operations: USAID [United States Agency for International Development], DoD [Department of Defense], and the Central Intelligence Agency."[19] Although expanding (and perhaps clarifying) chief of mission authority can contribute to unity of effort, this is not feasible in the near term given the ambiguity over the past sixty years, and legislation with respect to interagency reform is slow to move, if at all as is the case for The Interagency Cooperation Commission Act referenced earlier.

The previous paragraphs describe the aim of improving interagency processes is to achieve unity of effort and many view these changes as a key underpinning to interagency cooperation. Doctrine enlightens the dialogue by defining additional key terms. Joint Publication 1-02 defines *unity of effort* as "the coordination and cooperation toward common objectives, even if the participants are not necessarily part of the same command or organization."[20] Joint and Army doctrine uses different terms to describe how to achieve *unity of effort*. Joint doctrine describes *unity of effort* as a product of *unified action*, which is the synchronization, coordination, and/or integration of the activities of governmental and nongovernmental entities with military

---

[18] Lamb, "Expanding Chief of Mission Authority to Produce Unity of Effort," 6.

[19] Ibid.

[20] Joint Publication 1-02 (JP 1-02), 379.

operations to achieve unity of effort.[21] Army doctrine uses similar terms to achieve unity of

effort: *whole-of-government approach* or *comprehensive approach*. Field Manual 3-07 (Stability

Operations) defines a *whole-of-government approach* as "an approach that integrates the

collaborative efforts of the departments and agencies of the United States Government to achieve

unity of effort toward a shared goal."[22] A *comprehensive approach* is an "approach that integrates

the cooperative efforts of the departments and agencies of the United States Government,

intergovernmental and nongovernmental organizations, multinational partners, and private sector

entities to achieve unity of effort toward a shared goal."[23] Although there are several different

terms to describe how to achieve unity of effort, understanding the common thread of all these

definitions—integrating different government agencies toward a common goal—directly relate

back to our definition of *transition*[24]. History underscores another approach recently introduced

as another attempt to create unity of effort and a comprehensive approach.

The School of Military Government underpins another approach gaining traction

recently, which is the introduction of independent institutions to build certain capacities within

the military itself. The concept fully came to fruition in 1942, but it originated at the conclusion

of World War I by Colonel Irwin L. Hunt. Despite several military operations in other theaters

(e.g., Mexico in 1847–48 and the Spanish-American War) in which the United States Army

established military governments after the cessation of physical conflict, "in each instance,

---

[21] JP 1-02, 376.

[22] Army Field Manual 3-07 (FM 3-07), 1-4.

[23] Ibid.

[24] A transition is a point in time in which a distinct shift in focus and effort is required to achieve
strategic ends.

neither the Army nor the government accepted it as a legitimate military function."[25] This viewpoint changed after the Hunt Report where Hunt wrote, "the American army of occupation lacked both training and organization to guide the destinies of the nearly one million civilians whom the fortunes of war had placed under its temporary sovereignty."[26] After World War I, the military realized that "military government—the administration by military officers of civil government in occupied enemy territory—is a virtually inevitable concomitant of modern warfare."[27] After several revisions to doctrine and concepts that mirrored many of the other processes during the Interwar Period (1918–39), the School of Military Government opened on 11 May 1942 with fifty students.[28] This understanding of how war changed underpins why the discourse migrated towards reintroducing a similar concept in light of the nature of today's conflicts.

Carl J. Schramm is a chief proponent of reinstituting an approach similar to the School of Military Government to post-conflict operations. In the article "Expeditionary Economics," Schramm states, "It is imperative that the U.S. Military develop its competence in economics [and] establish a new field of inquiry that treats economic reconstruction as part of any successful three-legged strategy of invasion, stabilization or pacification, and economic reconstruction." [29] Schramm suggests the military "[build] an independent economic analytic capacity" paralleling the concept of the School of Military Government and the Armed Forces Institute of Pathology in

---

[25] Earl Frederick Ziemke, *The U.S. Army in the Occupation of Germany, 1944-1946*, Army Historical Series (Washington: Center of Military History, United States Army, 1975), 3.

[26] Ibid.

[27] Ibid.

[28] Ibid., 8.

[29] Carl J. Schramm, "Expedtionary Economics." *Foreign Affairs* May/June 2010, Vol 89, no. 3 (2010), 90.

his follow up article to "Expeditionary Economics." [30] The premise behind this independent, military-lead institute is essentially to develop economic theory "[guiding] action… [and bringing]…undeniable economic expansion" which Schramm agues is "critical to national security."[31] Schramm argues that an institute such as the "Armed Forces Institute on the Economics of Security and Strategy would be broad enough to include a variety of programs under its auspices" and its "focus would be on developing effective approaches to economic development in instances of American intervention, including pre-conflict (preventive defense), during conflict, and following conflict."[32] By doing so, the military would maintain the capacity to create conditions favorable for post-conflict environments.

The main problem with Schramm's approach is it is a parochial approach to war and does not contribute to achieving unity of effort. Schramm argues, "The United States has quite literally applied the whole of government in Iraq and Afghanistan, bringing the full force of the Federal bureaucracy."[33] Although increasing the military's ability to facilitate economic development in post-conflict environments is complimentary to current Joint and Army doctrine, it still ignores the whole-of-government approach and planning aspect necessary to implement the resultant theory effectively in operations. By concentrating on economics alone, the approach ignores other

---

[30] Carl J Schramm, "Institutionalizing Economic Analysis in the U.S. Military: The Basis for Preventive Defense," *Joint Forces Quarterly* 2nd Quarter 2011, no. 61, 35.

[31] Ibid., 38.

[32] Ibid.

[33] Ibid., 36.

elements of national power (primarily diplomatic and informational means) creating conditions

that do not emphasize the interdependence of these variables in the execution of war.[34]

The original intent behind the School of Military Government was to facilitate a

transition from the conflict and post-conflict environment led primarily by a military structure to

a post-conflict environment led primarily by civilian agencies. The type of a structure Schramm

argues for indirectly conflates the terms military-led and civilian-led and does not highlight their

interdependence. These terms are not to be exclusive of the other, but they do indicate primacy.

This is important to understand because it allows military planners to manage transitions. Using

the Operation Iraqi Freedom and New Dawn as an example, Operation Iraqi Freedom was a

military-led operation, but the U.S. Department of State and other government agencies were not

absent in Iraq. Organizations such as Provincial Reconstruction Teams worked in conjunction

with military counterparts to improve Iraqi security and stability. Operation New Dawn was a

civilian-led operation with a large military contingency. Even though there were still 50,000 U.S.

military personnel operating in Iraq, the Department of State was the lead U.S. government

agency and assumed greater responsibility over time. The U.S. military personnel continued to

retain much of the responsibility for the execution of established functions and structures mainly

because of the remaining enormity of the mission on 1 September 2011, but it was clear that the

United States Embassy–Baghdad, and not United States Forces–Iraq, was in the lead for

Operation New Dawn. There was a deliberate plan to facilitate the change from one operation to

another and transition from a military-led operation to a civilian-led one. Planning as a way to

_____

[34] Diplomatic, Information, Military, and Economic are the core elements of national power and the acronym DIME represents them. Another look at the elements of national power incorporates Financial Intelligence, and Law enforcement. The acronym MIDLIFE or DIMEFIL represents this look.

facilitate transitions and unity of effort probably receives the least amount of attention in the discourse despite it being one of the most important aspects.

The planning discussion revolves around the national level usually involving the National Command Authority. Mark Bucknam and Rick Swain both address planning aspects of the interagency processes, but from different perspectives. Bucknam analyzes planning from the national level examining the Adaptive Planning Initiative and the process it entails.[35] The key to his narrative is "planning compels interaction among military planners throughout DoD, and between those military planners and the staffs that support policymakers in the Pentagon."[36] This dialogue is also important to establish "clear strategic guidance."[37]

Correspondingly, Swain encourages a design methodology to improve interagency interaction using a 2009 interagency exercise in Europe to underpin his discussion.[38] He argues that "broadly understood techniques of design offer the best synthesis for achieving unity of effort in whole-of-government operations."[39] Swain's essay describes how the five main design questions aim to help in "reaching agreement on a common approach, acquiring a shared understanding of the crisis, and identifying the necessary operational level response" which is an important aspect to understanding complex environments.[40] The main reason why Swain

---

[35] Mark A. Bucknam, "Planning Is Everything," *Joint Forces Quarterly* 3rd Quarter, no. 62 (2011), 53. Secretary of Defense Donald Rumsfeld introduced the Adaptive Planning Initiative in 2003 to produce better plans more quickly. Secretary Gates continued this initiative.

[36] Ibid., 55.

[37] Ibid.

[38] Rick Swain, "Converging on Whole-of-Government Design," *Interagency Essay*, no. 11-01 (April 2011). http://thesimonscenter.org/wp-content/uploads/2011/04/IAE-11-01-April2011.pdf (accessed August 4, 2011), 2.

[39] Ibid.

[40] Ibid., 4. Swain states the five broad questions are: Why are we here? Where are we? Where do we want to go? How do we move from here to there? How shall we do that?

promotes design as a methodology is that "design properly seeks to describe how the whole-of-government will approach transforming the current situation by the harmonized actions of all agencies and other favorably interested parties."[41] The significance of Bucknam and Swain's arguments are the primacy of leveraging military planning expertise and synchronizing all elements of national power to achieve desired conditions. However, both concentrate on conceptual levels of planning omitting an approach for detailed planning.

Planning and its relation to transitions are important because the transition from military operations to civilian relationships underpins war termination. This is a key doctrinal concept. Termination is associated with the military end state and the preservation of achieved advantages toward the achievement of the national strategic end state.[42] The President and/or the Secretary of Defense approve termination criteria established by Joint Forces, which are the specified standards joint operations must meet before its termination.[43]

However, it is important to realize transition from military-led operations to civilian-led diplomatic relationships does not equate to war termination because even if the operation is civilian-led, this does not mean the war or conflict achieves the political ends. The distinction between Operations Iraqi Freedom and New Dawn is a key example. Operation Iraqi Freedom ended on 31 August 2010, however, the war and the overall Iraq Campaign continued until 14 December 2011—the date the national command authority announced as the campaign's end. This is also the date all operations associated with Operation New Dawn—military and civilian—ceased, the new bilateral relationship between the United States and Iraq started, and the

---

[41] Swain, "Converging on Whole-of-Government Design," 3.

[42] JP 5-0, xxi.

[43] JP 1-02, 359.

campaign objectives of Operation Iraqi Freedom and New Dawn achieved. In doctrinal terms, the transition from Operation Iraqi Freedom to New Dawn represents Phase IV (Stabilize) and Phase V (Enable Civil Authorities) operations found in the Joint Publication Phasing Model.[44] This is a doctrinal recognition that the transition between military and civilian authorities occurs before the overall military campaign terminates, but this transition also directly relates to war termination because if the transition materializes poorly, the achievement of strategic ends is doubtful. Although a transition and war termination can coincide at the same point in time, the two are not always the same.

Much of the dialogue to improve military operations focuses on the interagency processes or structure or developing institutions to increase capability and capacity. These debates have merit. An improved interagency process does facilitate an improved interaction and efficiency between the military and other government agencies to contribute to whole of government approaches and unity of effort. New institutions contribute to the body of knowledge within the military and build a better understanding of different theories to apply to complex environments. However, planning expertise and resources better integrate military efforts with other government agencies. The history of the United States offers several examples of transition that demonstrate how planning either facilitated or hindered effective transitions from military-led operations to civilian-led post-conflict environments.

History of Planning Transitions

The three cases studies (World War II, Vietnam, and Panama) use the process tracing methodology to reveal three primary characteristics: level of post-conflict planning prior to the

---

[44] JP 5-0, III-41.

15

conclusion of military operations, dialogue between military and civilian leadership, and transition criteria. World War II and the Vietnam War are the primary case studies. Panama and Operations Just Cause and Promote Liberty provide a look at a smaller, more recent conflict, but have similar challenges as with the larger conflicts. The first case study examined is Operation Eclipse in World War II.

On 22 May 1943, Lieutenant General Sir Frederick E. Morgan, Chief of Staff to Supreme Allied Command (COSSAC), and his planners started planning for the occupation of Germany upon its collapse under the codename Operation Rankin.[45] Operation Rankin focused on operations assuming a sudden German collapse during World War II. Operation Rankin planning occurred concurrently with two other planning efforts. The first was deception operations to reduce the German pressure on the western front, and the second was the invasion of the European continent. The former evolved into Operations Solitude and Fortress with the latter becoming Operation Overlord. Because planning occurred in the early stages of the European Theater of Operations, COSSAC planners faced several trials, but an early start to planning allowed them to work through issues prior to execution and identify important requirements.

One of the troubles planners faced was the lack of strategic guidance from American and British leadership and to a lesser degree, the Soviets. Allied leadership could not reach an agreement over several issues pertaining to Operations Solitude and Overlord, let alone coming to agreement of what a post-conflict Germany should look like.[46] There was also disagreement in

---

[45] Allied Expeditionary Force Supreme Headquarters, "History of Cossac (Chief of Staff to Supreme Allied Commander) 1944–1946," (Historical Sub-Section, Office of Secretary General Staff, May 1944). http://www history.army.mil/documents/cossac/Cossac.htm (accessed 25 October 2011), 21.

[46] United States Army, "Planning for the Occupation of Germany," (Frankfurt, Germany: Office of the Chief Historian, European Command, 1947).

the Roosevelt administration on the role of the armed forces in government administration and a lack of civil affairs trained personnel existed within the military to do so. In the absence of strategic guidance, Rankin planners drew from experiences at the end of World War I. Morgan stated, "The sum total of all the various factors now operating cannot be far from that of the factors which caused the collapse in 1918."[47] Using this assumption in combination with the early start to occupation planning enabled COSSAC planners to start coordinating for resources.

In addition to an initial supposition on the number of divisions required to occupy Germany, Rankin planners identified the need to establish military government in the occupied areas. The purpose of the military government would be to "preserve law and order, and to insure that the Force Commander's instruction in regard to security, disarmament, etc. are carried out."[48] The requirement for a military government exposed two additional requirements, which were that an early decision will be required for which policy to pursue; and the military government must appoint a Civil Affairs staff to make detailed plans for the establishment of military government and the rehabilitation of the country.[49] Because of the early identification of these needed resources, Rankin planners were able to open a dialogue with Allied leadership to start making preparations and enable continued planning for the occupation of Germany.

COSSAC planners divided Operation Rankin into three different scenarios named Rankin-A, Rankin-B, and Rankin-C. The primary plan, Rankin-C, assumed the unconditional surrender of Germany and planners identified this as the most likely scenario. Rankin-C's focus was narrow and assumed an unopposed movement into Germany as part of the unconditional

---

[47] Supreme Headquarters. *History of COSSAC*, 21.

[48] United States Army, "Planning for the Occupation of Germany," 15.

[49] United States Army, "The First Year of Occupation: Occupation Forces in Europe Series 1945-1946," (Frankfurt, Germany: Office of the Chief Historian, European Command, 1947).

surrender. As the war in Europe continued, Operation Rankin evolved into Operation Eclipse as COSSAC gave way to Supreme Headquarters Allied Expeditionary Force and Operation Overlord concluded. After the Overlord landings, it was apparent that an unopposed movement into Germany as part of the unconditional surrender was an invalid assumption and planning for Operation Talisman commenced in July 1944. On 30 October 1944, Talisman received a new codename—Eclipse—when the Allies received information leading them to believe the operational plan was compromised.

The focus for Eclipse was broader than that of Rankin and would commence upon the surrender of Germany and cessation of armed resistance. Eclipse would disarm Germany, implement the Allied occupation plan, and establish conditions that would enable the "United Nations agencies [to] assist in the relief and rehabilitation of liberated countries."[50] Rankin identified the initial requirements for Eclipse and Eclipse continued to refine those requirements as the conditions in Europe changed.

The Eclipse planning was significant for two reasons. First, Eclipse planners viewed the operation as a transitional period prior to civil control. Both COSSAC and Supreme Headquarters Allied Expeditionary Force planners understood the conditions for the occupation of Germany would require a military government to maintain order and conditions that allowed other governmental and international agencies to operate. Second, Operation Rankin initiated a process of thinking and planning for post conflict operations that would continue through the rest of the war. According to Kenneth McCreedy, Rankin and Eclipse planners "gained a greater appreciation for the complexity of the operation and the elements of post-conflict planning. Their

_____

[50] United States Army, "The First Year of Occupation: Occupation Forces in Europe Series 1945-1946," 58.

18

efforts forced military and political leaders to pause during their conduct of the war and briefly consider the shape of the peace they were pursuing."[51] These two factors lead to a successful transition in Europe.

The Operation Eclipse planning process reveals several key points. By starting the planning early even though the future environment was ambiguous, COSSAC planners established a dialogue with national leadership to exchange ideas that informed military planners of strategic aims. Early planning also allowed military planners to continuously update and refine the plan, so when implemented resources and structures were either already in place or were available in time to contribute to a successful transition from combat to a post-conflict environment.

In contrast to World War II Europe, the transition in Vietnam did not support the strategic ends. When President Richard M. Nixon announced his Vietnamization policy in 1969, which scheduled troop withdrawals as the South Vietnamese military "became strong enough to defend their country," Military Assistance Command Vietnam (MACV) planners already assumed troop withdrawal would occur soon and started incorporating the transition into planning.[52] MACV planners, under the command of General Creighton Abrams, instituted the "one war strategy" that targeted both the insurgent and the conventional forces fighting against South Vietnam. When General Abrams assumed command of MACV in July 1968, he directed a reevaluation of the Attrition Strategy. Abrams desired a "one war concept that does not recognize a separate war of

---

[51] Kenneth O. McCreedy, "Planning the Peace: Operation Eclipse and the Occupation of Germany," *Journal of Military History* 65, no. 3 (July 2001). http://www.jstor.org/stable/2677532 (accessed 23 August 2011), 72.

[52] Address by President Richard Nixon, November 3, 1969, Gareth Porter, ed, *Vietnam a History in Documents,* (New York, NY: Meridian Books, 1981), 386; Dave R. Palmer, *Summons of the Trumpet: U.S.-Vietnam in Perspective* (San Rafael, CA: Presidio Press, 1978), 219-220.

big battalions, war of pacification, or war of territorial security," but would "carry the battle to the enemy simultaneously, in all areas of conflict."[53] The one war strategy essentially followed three strategic thrusts—lines of effort in current doctrinal terms—to execute the war: the advisor mission, combat operations, and pacification.[54] Vietnamization encompassed these three strategic thrusts and essentially set the conditions for a transition from MACV to the South Vietnam military and a withdrawal of the United States military from South Vietnam. The Civil Operations and Revolutionary Development Support program (CORDS) was a major part of this effort.

President Lyndon B. Johnson initiated the CORDS program in 1967, and "assigned responsibility for counterinsurgency to the military and integrated all programs, including civilian, under its command."[55] According to the CORDS manual, its purpose was a "coordinated military and civil process to restore public security; initiate political, social, and economic development; extend Vietnamese Government authority; and win the support of the people."[56] In order to integrate both civilian and military processes adequately, the command structure reflected the one war strategy. For example, at MACV, overall command was under Abrams,

_____

[53] United States Military Assistance Command, Vietnam (MACV), "Commander's Summary of the MACV Objectives Plan," 1969, 22-23, Douglas Pike Collection, Texas Tech, http://www.virtualarchive.vietnam.ttu.edu (accessed 1 October 2008).

[54] Strategic Thrust: Power exerted in accordance with a strategy designed to move in a desired direction. The thrust may reduce the source of opposing political, economic, social, psychological, and military power, or it may enhance allied powers. "Combined Strategic Objectives Plan," January 1970, 11, Douglas Pike Collection, The Vietnam Center and Archive at Texas Tech University, Lubbock, TX, (hereafter referred as Texas Tech), http://www.virtualarchive.vietnam.ttu.edu (accessed 14 November 2011)

[55] Henry Nuzum, *Shades of CORDS in the Kush: The False Hope of Unity of Effort in American Counterinsurgency* (Carlisle, PA: Strategic Studies Institute, April 2010), viii.

[56] Military Assistance Command Vietnam Headquarters, "Assistant Chief of Staff, Cords Organization and Functions Manual," (Saigon, Vietnam: Military Assistance Command Vietnam, 1970), 5. Ambassador Komer preceded at CORDS original inception in 1967.

while the deputy (CORDS) was Ambassador Colby (3-star equivalent). Subordinate commands, such as Field Force II, reflected the MACV structure as well where the military was in command and a civilian was the deputy.[57] In other words, CORDS focused on pacification, which was supposed to develop loyalty and support for the South Vietnamese government at both the local and national levels, and had responsibility within the other two strategic thrusts (advisor mission and combat operations), but the military was still clearly in charge. At its peak, CORDS involved approximately 8,500 civilian and military advisors working with South Vietnamese counterparts.

Despite this integrated approach, which addressed the major issues facing MACV, the South Vietnamese government fell to the communist North Vietnamese in April 1975, two years after the signing of the Paris Accords in January 1973 and withdrawal of US forces from the south. Critics attribute some of this failure to the limited scope and duration of the CORDS program. Former Ambassador Komer attributes CORDS' failure on the overall Vietnam situation was because it was to too little, too late.[58] According to Komer, "even after 1967, pacification remained a small tail to the very large conventional military dog. It was never tried on a large enough scale until too late."[59] Another impediment to CORDS is that it did not address the ineffectiveness of the South Vietnamese government as a whole, especially at the national level, which was an important aspect of the Vietnamization program (in addition to building the effectiveness of the South Vietnamese armed forces).

---

[57] Ibid.

[58] Ross Coffey, "Revisiting Cords: The Need for Unity of Effort to Secure Victory in Iraq." *Military Review*, (March/April 2006), 32.

[59] Bruce Palmer, *The 25-Year War: America's Military Role in Vietnam*, A Da Capo Paperback (New York, N.Y.: Da Capo Press, 1990), 164.

In fact, MACV and CORDS inadequately addressed extending South Vietnamese governance as a key objective. A former CORDS analyst stated, "CORDS was a great program and a good model—with one caveat. Under the Hamlet Evaluation System, we collected lots of data indicating the security of the regions and provinces but nowhere did we find any evidence or indication of popular support of the [national-level] government."[60] Late implementation, limited scope, and lack of focus failed to link the strategic objectives of Vietnamization with the tactical actions of MACV, but there is an important lesson learned from CORDS.

Dale Andrade and LTC James H. Willbanks wrote the following about CORDS and the Vietnam War:

> Unity of effort is imperative; there must be a unified structure that combines [conventional] military and Pacification efforts. The Pacification program in Vietnam did not make any headway until the different agencies involved [came] together under a single manager with the military C2 architecture. Once CORDS… became part of the military chain of command it was easier to get things done. The military tends to regard Pacification as something civilian agencies do; however, only the military has the budget, material and manpower to get the job done … These lessons might seem obvious, and it is true that with hindsight, they might be easily identified; however, in practice, they are hard to execute.[61]

The point is CORDS, despite the overall outcome of the Vietnam War, had the potential to integrate efforts in Vietnam to establish conditions that would have met the overall objectives of Vietnamization.

A study of Vietnam reveals that although establishing an effective interagency structure facilitated a better overall military-civilian effort that the key aspects to effective transitions is an

---

[60] Ibid.

[61] Dale Andrade and LTC James H. Willbanks, "Cords/Phoenix Counterinsurgency Lessons from Vietnam for the Future," *Military Review* (March/April 2006). http://smallwarsjournal.com/documents/ milreviewmarch2.pdf (accessed 25 September 2011), 11.

early start and iterations to synchronize efforts. The concept of CORDS occurred in 1967, years

after U.S. involvement in Vietnam started and too late to affect war efforts. CORDS also did not

contribute to the achievement of the strategic ends associated with Vietnamization because it

lacked emphasis on the linkage between the South Vietnamese's local and national governments.

This late developing structure and lack of synchronization eventually led to a collapse of the

South Vietnamese government because of a lack of its perceived legitimacy and a poor bilateral

relationship between the U.S. and South Vietnamese that did not provide the latter with adequate

military or diplomatic support from the former.

Where Vietnam shows how delayed planning and disjointed objectives lead to poor

transitions, operations in Panama demonstrate that even though initiating planning early is

helpful, a lack of iteration and refinement can delay transitions. Operation Just Cause started on

20 December 1989 and was the culmination of a tumultuous relationship between General

Manuel Antonio Noriega, Panamanian dictator, and the United States Government in the 1980s.

Starting in 1987, tensions between the United States and Noriega grew as Noriega's anti-

American rhetoric increased and "at his direction, the [Panamanian Defense Forces initiated]

incidents of harassment against U.S. military personnel in the country, such as the arbitrary arrest

and detention of nine servicemen in October 1987."[62] Based on accusations from one of

Noriega's lieutenants, a U.S. grand jury indicted Noriega on drug trafficking charges in February

1988, which increased the frequency of U.S. service member harassment. From February 1988 to

December 1989, incidents against U.S. service members increased in frequency and intensity,

---

[62] R. Cody Phillips, *Operation Just Cause: The Incursion into Panama* (Washington: Center of Military History, United States Army), 5.

culminating in the fatal shooting of a Marine Corps lieutenant by the Panamanian Defense Forces and the detainment and assault of a U.S. Navy officer and his wife.

Operation Just Cause's objectives were "to safeguard the lives of Americans, to defend democracy in Panama, to combat drug trafficking, and to protect the integrity of the Panama Canal treaty," and President Bush later ordered the immediate apprehension and extradition of Noriega.[63] Operation Just Cause ended on 11 January 1990. Operation Promote Liberty followed, the stability and enabling civil authority operation, but for several weeks, these two operations overlapped.[64] The significance of Operation Just Cause is when planning started, how planning evolved over time, and how planners viewed the transition from combat to stability operations.

Planning for Operation Just Cause started in June 1987 as a response to anti-Noriega demonstrations.[65] As diplomatic and military relations between Panama and the United States deteriorated and the option of military force against Noriega increased, U.S. Southern Command (SOUTHCOM) increased planning efforts against the PDF. The original plan (dated 4 March 1988) that General Frederick F. Woerner, Jr. and SOUTHCOM presented the Joint Chiefs of Staff consisted of four phases. Planners referred to these four phases by code name Blue Spoon and later named Operation Just Cause. Yates describes that "the fourth, or combat, phase [in] the plan made clear the Noriega dictatorship would be a casualty of the operation—a 'regime change' in today's parlance."[66] However, the original plan did not plan for the restoration of the Panamanian government.

_____

[63] Ibid., 9.

[64] Lawerence Yates, "Panama, 1988-1989: The Disconnect between Combat and Stability Operations," *Military Review*, (May/June 2005): 46.

[65] Ibid.

[66] Ibid., 47.

Civil affairs officers in SOUTHCOM drafted a fifth phase to the operation—code name Blind Logic and later named Operation Promote Liberty—intended to "stabilize the situation and restore law and order until the new Panamanian government could function on its own."[67] Using World War II to underpin analysis, civil affairs planners assumed "that SOUTHCOM's commander would assume full political-military responsibility for U.S. interests in Panama once combat began and would preside over a military government for about 30 days."[68] This fifth phase would also set the conditions to gradually transition government functions from the U.S. military to the U.S. Embassy and the new Panamanian government. An early start to planning enabled SOUTHCOM to identify initial tasks and conditions necessary to facilitate a transition between the military and civilian counterparts, but conceptual planning was unfortunately also the extent of transition planning.

As planning for Operation Just Cause progressed, several problems arose. First, most of the civil affairs planners for Blind Logic were Army Reservists that rotated in and out of the planning cycle and never received full access to Blue Spoon.[69] Although planners were able to conceptualize the conditions necessary to start and end the fifth phase, they were never able to link those conditions with the combat phases. Second, the JCS never officially approved the fifth phase until the morning of the invasion.[70] Because Blind Logic was not officially approved, conversations between XVIII Airborne Corps and SOUTHCOM planners about the details on how to execute Blind Logic never materialized despite both sides recognizing U.S. military forces

---

[67] Ibid.

[68] Ibid.

[69] Ibid.

[70] Ibid., 46.

would encounter civil-military operations (CMO) after the cessation of combat. Lawrence Yates sums up the resultant situation as follows:

> On the eve of Operation Just Cause, then, disconnects still existed between the invasion plan and the CMO plan with respect to the conduct of stability operations. This meant the tactical units preparing to take part in the invasion concentrated on their combat roles, devoting little or no attention to the stability operations they would be called on to perform, which probably would have been the case even if coordination had been better during the planning phase.[71]

Even though Yates' last statement insinuates coordination would not have helped the transition between Operations Just Cause and Promote Liberty, the previous Eclipse and Vietnam examples disprove his circumstantial claim by demonstrating coordination does in fact contribute to better transitions. Despite these setbacks, U.S. government and military reacted quickly to avoid disaster after hostilities ceased. Operation Promote Liberty continued until the end of 1990.

The Panama study shows SOUTHCOM planners were diligent in their recognition of a lack of stability operations phase and their subsequent planning. National leadership quickly approved Operation Promote Liberty because the early start on Blind Logic (Promote Liberty) planning helped establish a conceptual framework that coordinated needed resources, mainly military police and civil affairs soldiers, to restore control and order after the cessation of combat operations in Operation Just Cause. However, the lack of integration and refinement between Blue Spoon (Just Cause) and Blind Logic (Promote Liberty) and between key civilian and military personnel led to the delayed coordination of the proper resources to support the transition from military to civilian personnel to defend democracy in Panama, a specified strategic objective.

---

[71] Ibid., 50.

What Makes a Successful Transition?

The previous cases studies suggest three characteristics to support successful transitions: level of post-conflict planning prior to the conclusion of military operations, dialogue between planners not only within the military, but also between the military and the interagency community, and refinements made to the plan to establish transition criteria. The symbiotic relationship between these three characteristics reveals that early planning facilitates an open and iterative dialogue between military planners and civilian officials. This discourse then reveals the necessary requirements and end state conditions to transition operations from the military to civilian agencies. As conditions and requirements changes, planners are able to make refinements to the plan, thus allowing for a successful transition later.

Early planning is the foundation for planning a successful transition. Fred C. Iklé states, "The grand design is often woefully incomplete. Usually, in fact, it is not grand enough: most of the exertion is devoted to the means—perfecting the military instruments and deciding on their use in battles and campaigns—and far too little is left for relating these means to their ends."[72] He further explains, "While skillfully planning their intricate operations and coordinating complicated maneuvers, [military planners] remain curiously blind in failing to perceive that it is the outcome of the war, not the outcome of the campaigns within it, which determines how well their plans serve the nation's interests."[73] In other words, the military must consider what the post-conflict environment looks like to not only prepare for the cessation of hostilities, but, also, to understand how to support the overall national level objectives of the war. Iklé's statements not only highlight the importance of war termination criteria, but also imply military planners need to

---

[72] Fred Charles Iklé, *Every War Must End* (New York: Columbia University Press, 1971), 1.
[73] Ibid., 2.

understand how to reestablish the political dialogue between warring nations. Comparing and contrasting the three case studies in relation to the criteria of early planning will highlight this concept.

All three historical examples—Operation Eclipse, Vietnam, and Operation Just Cause—feature instances of early planning. Transition planning during World War II started in 1942 while combat operations just commenced for the Allies (with the addition of the United States). Operation Rankin planners anticipated three different scenarios—unconditional surrender, rapid collapse of Germany enabling an early execution of Operation Overlord, and a contraction of German force to pre-war borders—two of which would require a transition from combat operations to a post-conflict environment. Operation Just Cause, similar to World War II planning, anticipated a fifth phase for a post-conflict environment. In fact, World War II underpinned Blind Logic (Operation Promote Liberty) planning as a framework for the transition. During the Vietnam War, MACV planners assumed an American withdrawal was pending two years prior to the Nixon Administration announcing the Vietnamization policy in 1969. Despite these similarities, the outcome of the transitions differed to varying degrees because of a variety of reasons.

A significant difference between Operation Eclipse (Rankin), Operation Just Cause, and Vietnam, was at which point planning for a transition started. Operation Eclipse planning started at the onset of U.S. operations in World War II under the auspice of a Europe first strategy and unconditional surrender of Germany (and Japan). Operation Just Cause transition planning started two years prior (1987) to any actual military action occurring because as tensions with Noriega increased, SOUTHCOM anticipated military action to "defend democracy in Panama." Each started either prior to or at the start of the conflict with a generally expressed end state condition.

On the other hand, transition planning in Vietnam started much closer to the end than the beginning of the conflict. As stated earlier, the MACV planners assumed a U.S. military withdrawal in 1967, but did not start serious transition planning until 1969 and the announcement of Vietnamization. Second, the finalization of the CORDS program, which involved personnel required, command and control structures, and enduring programs, did not occur until 1967—four years after the start of the war. Finally, MACV and CORDS's execution of Vietnamization, might have been successful developing regional and local levels and training the South Vietnamese armed forces, but failed to link these successes with the overall strategic situation or desired conditions (i.e., extending South Vietnamese governance). MACV planners failed to address how to transition the South Vietnamese armed forces without U.S. aid and linking the South Vietnamese national-level government with the local and regional governments which eventually led to the collapse of its armed forces, unification of Vietnam under communist rule, and virtually no diplomatic relations between the United States and Vietnam in 1975. Thomas M. Bibby describes the situation in 1975 in *Vietnam: The End, 1975*.

> The United States taught the South Vietnamese armed forces well on how to fight and win a conventional war against the North Vietnamese; however, the U.S. taught them the American way, with massive firepower and plenty of mobility (i.e., artillery, air and helicopters) that could only be supported by continued U.S. aid--something a war-weary U.S. public and Congress were unwilling to fund .... Indeed, if Vietnamization had any chance at all in being successful in 1975, it was thwarted by Congress' withholding of two vital prerequisites: U.S. air support and military aid. However, there were serious problems within the South Vietnam government which acted to erode American public and Congressional support. These internal problems ultimately brought about the collapse of the South Vietnamese armed forces. [74]

Early transition planning enables military planners to open a dialogue with their civilian counterparts to not only identify requirements early, but to ensure a linkage between military actions and political aims.

---

[74] Thomas M Bibby, "Vietnam: The End, 1975," *Small Wars Journal* (1985). http://smallwarsjournal.com/documents/bibby.pdf (accessed 25 October 2011), 61-62.

Early planning also facilitates developing a shared understanding and consensus. Iklé explains in *Every War Must End* that:

> In preparing a major military operation, military leaders and civilian officials can effectively work together in large teams to create a well-meshed, integrated plan. This holds true, almost regardless of how well or how badly the war is going. By contrast, planning to end a war where victory seems out of reach is not a task on which men can easily collaborate. To search for an exit in such a situation, government leaders can rarely move in harmony.[75]

Although the events revolving around the Vietnam War frame Iklé's statements, the greater significance is that to come to a consensus between the military and policy makers when it comes to ending a war is challenging. If early planning underpins a successful transition, then the iterative revisions of the plan create opportunities for discourse between military and civilian leaders, which increases the chances of setting necessary conditions for a successful transition. The three case studies, again, highlight this point to varying degrees.

In the case of Operation Eclipse, COSSAC planners first presented Rankin to President Roosevelt and Prime Minister Churchill during the Quebec Conference in August 1943. Although Roosevelt or Churchill made no direct decisions at the end of this conference other than to continue transition planning, the presentation of Rankin at the conference opened a discourse between military and civilian leaders that would later shape the outcome of Operation Eclipse and the execution of the occupation of Germany. In other words, the planning done by the military opened a discourse not only between military and civilian leaders, but also between political leaders, which in turn developed nascent U.S. policies with respect to the transition from war to peace. For example, Joint Chiefs of Staff directive 1067 (JCS 1067) originated through discussions between Eclipse planners and the War Department of what the political and economic

---

[75] Iklé, *Every War Must End*, 85.

conditions of a surrendering Germany would be and what the post-conflict command and control structure would be. The Morgenthau Plan, which proposed measures to limit Germany's ability to wage war, also informed how JCS 1067 was developed. When published in April 1945, JSC 1067 stated "No action will be taken in execution of the reparations program or otherwise which would tend to support basic living conditions in Germany or in your zone on a higher level than that existing in any one of the neighboring United Nations."[76] In other words, occupying forces made improvements to basic life support systems, but nothing else. Since COSSAC and SHAEF planners started transition planning early in the conflict, discourse between military and civilian leadership contributed to the overall success of the transition upon unconditional surrender of Germany.

Those involved with MACV and CORDS failed to reframe the problem in Vietnam after Nixon announced the Vietnamization policy and this caused an incoherent dialogue between military and civilian leaders. According to Nixon, "[Vietnamization is] a plan in which we will withdraw all our forces from Vietnam on a schedule in accordance with our program, as the South Vietnamese become strong enough to defend their own freedom."[77] As mentioned before, MACV implemented a "one war strategy" consisting of three strategic thrusts (combat operations, advisor mission, and pacification) and Vietnamization was a compilation of the three. Although the plan called for three strategic thrusts, the military planners and Nixon administration talked about combat, not about the other elements necessary to implement Vietnamization fully. Pacification sought "to establish cooperation among the people, between

---

[76] Joint Chiefs of Staff, Directive to Commander-in-Chief of United States Forces of Occupation Regarding the Military Government of Germany, April 1945, http://usa.usembassy.de/etexts/ga3-450426.pdf (accessed 1 October 2011), 3.

[77] Nixon Vietnamization Speech, November 3, 1969.

the people and the government, and among the various government agencies," but rarely discussed this factor to transition from U.S. primacy to South Vietnamese primacy.[78] In part, because MACV's "one war strategy" implemented the framework (the CORDS structure and the Vietnamization policy) late in the war, military planners were unable to change the dialogue and to anticipate the emergent conditions to implement Vietnamization fully and did not extend South Vietnamese governance.

In the case of Operation Just Cause, a dialogue between the military and civilian leadership opened because of early planning, but the dialogue was limited and diminished as the conflict became unavoidable. Planners developed a relatively complete conceptual framework for Blind Logic, the fifth phase dealing with the post-conflict environment. The failure occurred because of the limited scope of those involved and an over concentration on combat planning. Phillips states, "Only a small number of senior commanders and staff officers were aware of a possible military intervention."[79] When combined with the rotation of civil affairs reservists with limited knowledge of the other four combat phases, transitioning between combat and post-combat environments became difficult. Despite this limited dialogue and lack of detailed planning of Blind Logic, by the beginning of January 1990, "all the emergency needs had been addressed. Civil affairs teams were operating throughout the country, providing training for local officials and coordinating various domestic services" and by 12 January 1990, Operation Just Cause officially ended.[80]

---

[78] Office of the Deputy for CORDS, Headquarters, II Field Force Vietnam, "1970 Pacification and Development Program," (Saigon, SVN: MACV, 1970), 1.

[79] Phillips, *Operation Just Cause: The Incursion into Panama*, 11.

[80] Ibid., 44.

Conrad C. Crane describes "transition operations ... as military forces [trying] to position the area of operation to move back to peace and under the control of civilian government."[81] He further describes that the part of post-conflict operations most problematic for military forces is "the handover to civilian agencies."[82] So far, the analysis describes how early planning facilitates a dialogue between military planners and policy makers. These characteristics lead to the remaining ones, which are the identification of necessary conditions and the continuous refinement of the plan to facilitate a successful transition.

Initially, the COSSAC planners received very little strategic guidance, but the COSSAC and subsequently SHAEF planners continued to identify needed requirements and conditions for a post-conflict Germany. By doing this, not only did Allied planners shape how the post-conflict environment would be resourced, but also as discussed earlier, helped shape, and in some cases define, strategic guidance. During Rankin planning, COSSAC planners identified the need for a military government and lack of civil affairs expertise on the staff. COSSAC leadership brought these requirements to the Quebec Conference in 1943, and, in response, officials placed greater emphasis upon the School of Military Government and established a civil affairs section for future planning in Europe.[83] In addition to the allocation of resources, other requirements such as displaced persons, disarmament procedures, number of divisions required for the occupation, and

---

[81] Conrad C. Crane, "Phase IV Operations: Where Wars Are Really Won" in *Turning Victory into Success*, ed. Brian M. De Toy (Fort Leavenworth, KS: Combat Studies Institute Press) (2004), 1.

[82] Ibid.

[83] Ziemke, 7. The largest item of expense, professional personnel, was $11,000 in 1942, and the total budget for 1943 was $98,680, 17 increased somewhat by expansion during the year. (17) The Rhineland occupation after World War I, which only involved a population of about one million, required 213 military government officers, or .1 percent of the occupation force. On this basis, the study showed, an Army of four million men, without any allowance for the larger civilian population to lie governed, would need 4,000 officers, as many as the School of Military Government could produce in ten years (8)

requirements of the military government after occupation. Furthermore, the conditions in which the occupation would occur refined the plan. As mentioned previously, Rankin planning started with three different scenarios (Rankin A, Rankin B, and Rankin C). After Operations Overlord and Market Garden and because of changes in the European environment, SHAEF planners focused on Rankin-C (the unconditional surrender of Germany). Once the unconditional surrender of Germany occurred, Operation Eclipse established a well-thought out plan to establish and create the conditions for transition from combat to a military government and eventually to a more normal diplomatic relationship with Germany after World War II.

MACV and CORDS planners failed to identify and establish the necessary conditions to transition responsibility from the United States to South Vietnam and extend its governance. Where Eclipse planners started planning early, opened a dialogue with national leaders (i.e., Roosevelt, Churchill, Marshall), and helped identify and define the conditions necessary to transition from military led operations to a civilian-led relationship, MACV failed to do so especially in the realm of defining the transition. The different opinions by those involved highlight the disparity between the American and South Vietnamese point of view. General William Westmoreland (Chief of Staff of the Army) highlights the American perception after the Easter Offensive of 1972 by saying, "Here … was the ultimate test of the long years of American effort to create viable South Vietnamese armed forces and of the decision taken … to organize regular units rather than light anti-guerrilla forces."[84] General Cao Van Vien (Chairman of the South Vietnamese Joint General Staff in 1972) said of the same operation:

> The enemy's offensive of 1972 dramatically brought to the surface the basic weakness of the Vietnamization process. Without U.S. support in airpower and mobility, the Republic

---

[84] Thomas M Bibby. "Vietnam: The End, 1975." *Small Wars Journal* (1985). http://smallwarsjournal.com/documents/bibby.pdf (accessed 25 October 2011), 60.

of Vietnam armed forces could hardly have held An Loc, defended Kontum, or reoccupied Quang Tri.[85]

An overreliance on American enablers coupled with a national government—riddled with corruption—not linked with the regional and local governments in the pacification program created conditions for a Vietnamese reunification under communist rule.

In Panama, SOUTHCOM and XVIII Airborne Corps planners failed to conduct detailed planning for post-conflict operations, but the conceptual planning completed prior allowed for some agility needed after combat operations ceased. The Joint Chiefs of Staff approved Operation Promote Liberty on 20 December 1998 and by 22 December, the initial civil affairs personnel started to flow in to Panama.[86] Planners failed to integrate the transition fully and thus it was not seamless during the operation. Once U.S. Forces neutralized the Panamanian Defense Forces, one of the shortcomings of the transition was the lack of public security. The XVIII Airborne Corps and Panamanian officials improvised to restore order by utilizing the new government to recruit a new police force. The lack of integration led to Operation Promote Liberty lasting longer than necessary.

Recommendations

The case studies on World War II, Vietnam, and Panama advocate that early planning, iterative engagements between military planners and civilian officials, and continuous refinements establish the conditions to successfully transition operations to a civilian-led diplomatic relationship. As Operation Enduring Freedom approaches its conclusion, these

---

[85] Arnold R. Isaacs, *Without Honor* (Baltimore and London: The Johns Hopkins University Press, 1983), 301.

[86] Phillips, *Operation Just Cause: The Incursion into Panama* ,43.

historical examples provide planners with potential approaches so that the U.S. Government achieves its strategic aims in 2014.

Doctrine provides a starting point from which to expand. Joint Publications define terms such as transition, termination, and phasing. Much like the shift from Operation Iraqi Freedom to Operation New Dawn signified a significant shift in effort and focus from military-led operations to civilian-led ones, a similar approach in Afghanistan can be of use. A similar phasing and transition concept represents to those contributing to Operation Enduring Freedom conditions are moving towards the accomplishment of strategic ends. It can also communicate publicly in the international arena the end of combat operations and a movement towards a more normal relationship with the Government of Afghanistan much like the end of Operation Iraqi Freedom indicated the end of combat operations in Iraq. Defining a transition as a point in time in which a distinct shift in focus and effort is required to achieve strategic ends. Changing structures may help, but identifying enduring functions and requirements for transitions requires planning.

Concepts such as whole of government approaches, interagency cooperation, and independent, military-led government institutions enter the discussion as ways to facilitate effective transitions. The focus of interagency cooperation is to achieve unity of effort. Independent government institutions build greater capacity within the military to affect other elements of national power such as economic, and this would maintain the capacity to create conditions favorable for post-conflict environments. The problem with these approaches is the lack of integration. Solving these problems may contribute to addressing the desire to achieve unity of effort, but if planning does not synchronize, coordinate, and integrate these elements, success is doubtful. The three historical case studies highlighted these issues, so what does it mean for current and future operations?

There are several implications for Afghanistan contained within these examples. If Afghanistan planners are to link tactical actions to strategic objectives to conclude Operation Enduring Freedom by 2014, there are three key recommendations. First, initiating transition

36

planning now to identify enduring functions, resources needed to maintain these functions, and initiate actions to ensure these resources are available in 2014 or before. Much like Operation Eclipse planning identified a lack of resources for a military government initiated additional training; early planning helps Afghanistan planners. It will enable them to start coordination for not only military, but also need civilian resources to continue critical functions past 2014.

Early planning enables the discourse between other planners and civilian counterparts to define conditions, identify requirements, and inform current operations. In order to facilitate transitions for Operation Enduring Freedom, planners must start early to initiate the cognitive discourse involved. As Iklé mentions in *Every War Must End*, consensus becomes harder to achieve as the war draws closer to the end and especially if success seems unlikely. Early planning forces the military and civilian leadership in Afghanistan to prioritize the right efforts and functions to focus on as time and resources start to diminish. Planners for Europe in World War II started almost immediately upon entering the war and developed a transition plan that facilitated a handoff to civilian authorities. The School of Military Government and post-conflict personnel structures were by-products of early planning. The former did not drive the latter.

Many times, strategic guidance is ambiguous and does not facilitate military planning, as may be the case in Afghanistan. End state conditions such as "self-reliant" are ambiguous, but Everett Dolmans states, "The strategist is comfortable with the knowledge that rules are constantly in flux, and instead of matching capabilities to ends within given limits, acts to modify the limits."[87] It is incumbent upon those military planners to initiate the dialogue with civilian counterparts to clarify strategic guidance, define the conditions that support that guidance, and

---

[87] Everett C. Dolman, *Pure Strategy Power and Principle in the Space and Information Age.* (New York: Routledge, 2005), 77.

use that information to inform current operations to set those conditions, or at minimum, intermediate conditions. After several iterations between COSSAC planners with political leadership (Roosevelt, Churchill, Marshall), Operation Eclipse fully defined "unconditional surrender of Germany." In 1942, COSSAC planners were operating mostly on assumptions, but by 1945, it was completely clear to those units operating in the European Theater of Operations what "unconditional surrender" entailed. If there is still doubt to what the strategic ends in Afghanistan are or mean, defining them now eliminates ambiguity in strategic guidance and enables actions in Afghanistan to move towards accomplishment of strategic aims.

Finally, planners should refine the plan to achieve the desired conditions. In other words, transition the plan from the conceptual plan to the detailed plan so that it can be executed and achieve strategic aims. This may seem self-evident, but if planning and dialogue are not initiated, then detailed planning will be inadequate if completed at all. In planning for Operation Just Cause and Promote Liberty, a lack of discourse failed to flesh out Blind Logic and the Joint Chiefs of Staff did not approve the plan until it was evident resources allocated to XVIII Airborne Corps were insufficient to maintain peace after hostilities ceased.

Conclusion

Clausewitz states, "War is merely the continuation of policy by other means."[88] This statement inextricably links the Department of Defense with other government agencies. It also means the military is always a viable option for our government to enforce policy and protect our national interests. The Department of Defense forms the largest portion of the government's discretionary spending. Even with budget cuts and the conclusion of Operation Enduring

---

[88] Carl von Clausewitz, *On War*, ed. Michael Howard and Peter Paret (Princeton: Princeton University Press, 1976), 87.

Freedom approaching, defense spending will remain larger than other government agencies such as the Department of State for the near future as national security and vital national interests remain at the forefront of national debates.

As the end of Operation Enduring Freedom approaches in the near future, the United States continues to develop Afghan security forces to become self-reliant. The same questions confronted in Iraq are the same ones planners in Afghanistan are struggling with today. Where the questions in Iraq deal with "did Operation New Dawn achieve the strategic objectives of a sovereign, stable, and self-reliant Iraq," the questions about Afghanistan are "how can Operation Enduring Freedom achieve the strategic aims of a self-reliant security force linked with an effective national government?" Time will reveal the successes and failures of Operation New Dawn as Iraq and its people continue to develop as a parliamentary democracy in the Middle East. However, it is critical for military planners in Afghanistan to initiate the conversations with civilian counterparts who will assume responsibility for those enduring military functions after 2014 to ensure achievement of strategic ends and the diplomatic relationship that follows is enduring. With approximately two years remaining before military operations end, Afghanistan is approximately at the same point in time Eclipse and Just Cause planners were when they initiated planning. This monograph demonstrates two years is enough time to start planning, facilitate a dialogue between military and civilian leadership, and refine a plan that creates conditions that effectively enable a successful transition from military-led operations to a civilian-led diplomatic relationship in a post-conflict environment.

Bibliography

12th Army Group. *Report of Operations (Final after Action Review)*, 31 July 1945. Vol. I: Summary.

Allied Expeditionary Force Supreme Headquarters. *Eclipse Memorandum 1: Appreciation and Outline Plan*, 25 April 1945. http://cgsc.contentdm.oclc.org/cdm/singleitem/collection/p4013coll8/id/501 (accessed 28 September 2011).

Andrade, Dale, and LTC James H. Willbanks. "CORDS/Phoenix Counterinsurgency Lessons from Vietnam for the Future." *Military Review* (March/April 2006). http://smallwarsjournal.com/documents/milreviewmarch2.pdf (accessed 25 September 2011).

BDM Corporation. *A Study of Strategic Lessons Learned in Vietnam*. Vol. II: South Vietnam. Alexandria, VA: Defense Logistics Agency, 1980.

Bibby, Thomas M. "Vietnam: The End, 1975." *Small Wars Journal* (1985). http://smallwarsjournal.com/documents/bibby.pdf (accessed 25 October 2011).

Bogdanos, Matthew E. "Joint Interagency Cooperation: The First Step." *Joint Forces Quarterly*, no. 37 (2005). http://www.au.af.mil/au/awc/awcgate/jfq/0437.pdf (accessed 1 October 2011).

Bucknam, Mark A. "Planning Is Everything." *Joint Forces Quarterly* 3rd Quarter 2011, no. 62 (2011): 52-58.

Clausewitz, Carl von. *On War*, Edited by Michael Howard and Peter Paret. Princeton: Princeton University Press, 1976.

Coffey, Ross. "Revisiting CORDS: The Need for Unity of Effort to Secure Victory in Iraq." *Military Review*, (March/April 2006): 24-36.

Crane, Conrad C. "Phase IV Operations: Where Wars Are Really Won" in *Turning Victory into Success*, edited by Brian M. De Toy, 1-22. Fort Leavenworth, KS: Combat Studies Institute Press 2004.

Davis, William J. "Is a Sense of Community Vital to Interagency Coordination?" *Interagency Paper*, no. 3 (January 2011).

Demboski, Richard K. "Eating Dinner with a Fork, Spoon, and Knife: How a Corps Executed MACV's One War Strategy." Master's Thesis, School of Advanced Military Studies, 2009.

Department of the Army. Field Manual 3-07: *Stability Operations*. Washington, D.C.: Department of the Army, October 2008.

Dolman, Carl Everett. *Pure Strategy: Power and Principle in the Space and Information Age*. New York: Routledge, 2005.

Fishel, John T. *The Fog of Peace: Planning and Executing the Restoration of Panama*. Carlisle Barracks, Pa.: Strategic Studies Institute, U.S. Army War College, 1992.

Headquarters, Military Assistance Command Vietnam "Assistant Chief of Staff, CORDS Organization and Functions Manual." Saigon, Vietnam: Military Assistance Command Vietnam, 1970.

Iklé, Fred Charles. *Every War Must End*. New York: Columbia University Press, 1971.

Isaacs, Arnold R. *Without Honor*. Baltimore and London: The Johns Hopkins University Press, 1983.

Komer, R. W., and United States Advanced Research Projects Agency. *Bureaucracy Does Its Thing: Institutional Constraints on U.S.-Gvn Performance in Vietnam*. Santa Monica,California: RAND, 1972. http://www.rand.org/content/dam/rand/pubs/reports/2005/R967.pdf (accessed 1 October 2011).

Lamb, Christopher, and Edward Marks. "Expanding Chief of Mission Authority to Produce Unity of Effort." *Interagency Essay*, no. 11-02 (May 2011). http://thesimonscenter.org/wp-content/uploads/2011/05/IAE-11-02-MAY2011.pdf (accessed August 4, 2011).

McCreedy, Kenneth O. "Planning the Peace: Operation Eclipse and the Occupation of Germany." Master's Thesis, School of Advanced Military Studies, 1995.

————. "Planning the Peace: Operation Eclipse and the Occupation of Germany." *Journal of Military History* 65, no. 3 (July 2001). http://www.jstor.org/stable/2677532 (accessed 23 August 2011).

Nuzum, Henry. *Shades of Cords in the Kush: The False Hope of Unity of Effort in American Counterinsurgency*. Carlisle, PA: Strategic Studies Institute, April 2010.

Obama, Barack. "Responsibly Ending the War in Iraq." In *Remarks of President Barack Obama* Camp Lejeune, North Carolina, 27 February 2009,

————. *Remarks by the President and First Lady on the End of the War in Iraq*, Fort Bragg, North Carolina. 14 December 2011.

Organisation for Economic Co-operation Development. "Whole of Government Approaches to Fragile States." edited by OECD Development Assistance Committee's Fragile States Group, 2006.

Palmer, Bruce. *The 25-Year War: America's Military Role in Vietnam*. A Da Capo Paperback. New York, N.Y.: Da Capo Press, 1990.

Phillips, R. Cody. *Operation Just Cause: The Incursion into Panama*. Washington: Center of Military History, United States Army.

Schramm, Carl J. "Expeditionary Economics." *Foreign Affairs* May/June 2010, Vol 89, no. 3 (2010): 89-99.

———. "Institutionalizing Economic Analysis in the U.S. Military: The Basis for Preventive Defense." *Joint Forces Quarterly* 2nd Quarter 2011, no. 61 (2011): 32-38.

Schwarzenberg, Jan. "Where Are the JIACGS Today?" *Interagency Journal* 2, no. 2 (Summer 2011): 24-32.

Sigal, Leon V. "A War without End." *World Policy Journal*, (2007): 1-8.

Joint Chiefs of Staff. *Directive to Commander-in-Chief of United States Forces of Occupation Regarding the Military Government of Germany*. http://usa.usembassy.de/etexts/ga3-450426.pdf , (accessed 1 October 2011).

———. Joint Publication 1-02, *Department of Defense Dictionary of Military and Associated Terms*. Washington, DC: Department of Defense, 15 July 2011.

———. Joint Publication 3-0, *Joint Operations*. Washington, DC: Department of Defense, 11 August 2011.

———. Joint Publication 5-0, *Joint Operations Planning*. Washington, DC: Department of Defense, 11 August 2011.

Supreme Headquarters, Allied Expeditionary Force. *History of Cossac (Chief of Staff to Supreme Allied Commander) 1944-1946*: Historical Sub-Section, Office of Secretary General Staff, May 1944. http://www.history.army.mil/documents/cossac/Cossac.htm (accessed 25 October 2011).

Swain, Rick. "Converging on Whole-of-Government Design." *Interagency Essay*, no. 11-01 (April 2011). http://thesimonscenter.org/wp-content/uploads/2011/04/IAE-11-01-April2011.pdf (accessed August 4, 2011).

Ulin, Bob. "About Interagency Cooperation." *Interagency Essay*, no. 10-01 (September 2010). http://thesimonscenter.org/wp-content/uploads/2010/09/IAE-10-01.pdf (accessed August 4, 2011).

United States Army. "The First Year of Occupation: Occupation Forces in Europe Series 1945-1946." Frankfurt, Germany: Office of the Chief Historian, European Command, 1947.

———. "Planning for the Occupation of Germany." Frankfurt, Germany: Office of the Chief Historian, European Command, 1947.

United States Government, "White Paper of the Interagency Policy Group's Report on U.S. Policy toward Afghanistan and Pakistan." http://www.whitehouse.gov/assets/documents/afghanistan_pakistan_white_paper_final.pdf (accessed 5 November 2011).

Yates, Lawerence. "Panama, 1988-1989: The Disconnect between Combat and Stability Operations." *Military Review*, (May/June 2005): 46-52.

Ziemke, Earl Frederick. *The U.S. Army in the Occupation of Germany, 1944-1946* Army Historical Series. Washington: Center of Military History, United States Army, 1975. http://www.history.army.mil/books/wwii/Occ-GY/, (accessed 1 October 2011).

www.ingramcontent.com/pod-product-compliance
Lightning Source LLC
Chambersburg PA
CBHW081758280526
45789CB00008B/2905